DISTANT SURVIVORS

A Poetic Drama
by June Prager
Adapted from the Poetry of William Heyen

Published by

Blue Moon Press

A Once-In-A –Blue-Moon Experience

For production information, contact Blue Moon Plays at
bluemoonstageplays@cox.net or phone 1-757-816-1164
or www.bluemoonplays.com

For all other inquiries, please contact June Prager, Mirage Theatre Company, juneprager.mirage@gmail.com

ISBN: 978-1-943416-13-4
Published by Blue Moon Plays
Virginia Beach, VA 23462
Cover Design by Maggie Douglas
Printed in the USA

DISTANT SURVIVORS

CAST:

Man .... 40's American of German descent; wears jeans, shirt, and lightweight jacket

Caretaker .... 50's – 60's Eastern European Jewish survivor; wears work pants, shirt, and cap

NS .... 50's – 60's; Nazi Soldier; wears Nazi helmet, white shirt and tie, SS uniform jacket, black pants, and black boots

Man 2 .... 60's – 70's; German Jewish survivor; wears dark brown suit

Woman .... 50's – 60's; Eastern European Jewish survivor; wears long skirt, top, and shawl

Time: 1990's
Place: Bremerhaven, Germany
Set: Stage R - a stool; Stage RC – a ladder; Stage C – a bench; Stage L – a small black platform (or black cubes)

Lighting: white and steely blue
Pre-set: on bench and dock area

House music: Eastern European folk music; begins about 10 minutes prior to starting time

SCENE ONE: Bremerhaven

House music fades and house lights go out.
LIGHTS: The bench and dock area comes up to full. The
Man enters from Stage R, moving toward platform area.
He's holding a map.

MAN:
Canes and armless coats
haunt these German streets
I force myself to walk.
Factories smoke the sky....

A few days ago,
I saw those Bremerhaven graves.
Unadorned stones
honor our simpler dust.
I almost knelt to save
a leaf of ivy. I even heard
the dead were glad
that I'd returned.

>   *Man climbs up onto the platform.   He moves to its*
>   *edge and looks out.*

The line of WWI veterans,
My mother's father among them,
stood at attention on a Bremerhaven dock.

Gusts of brine wind lapped
at the Fuhrer's black leather coat,
but he took his time,
took each man's hands in his own,
thanked each for his sacrifice.

He of the luminous wounded blue eyes,
seeing my grandfather's
prisoner-of-war medal, asked where,
& how long. "Russia, two years,"
my grandfather answered,
then added, "I escaped."

His beloved Fuhrer embraced him
in moments of blue flame.

Behind them, *Das Reich,*
their new battleship, loomed.

For the first time, a woman is allowed to see
her wounded husband, brought back from the East.
She finds him mutilated, missing an ear,
half his face, an arm. "It's the Jews,"
she screams. "it's all the Jews' fault."

> ***Man comes off the platform and sits down on bench.***
> ***He looks out toward the audience.***

Born in Brooklyn of German parents
I remember lines scratched on our doors,
the crooked swastikas my father cursed
and painted over.

They appeared, overnight,
on our steps, like frost stars
on our windows, their strict
crooked arms pointing
this way and that, scare-
crows, skeletons, limbs
akimbo.

My father
cursed in his other tongue
and scraped them off,
or painted them over.
My mother bit her lips.

And I remember
the *Volksfest* at Franklin Square
on Long Island every summer –
smoked eel, loaves of dark bread

raffles, shooting galleries,
beer halls, bowling alleys,
boys in *Lederhosen*
flooded by an ocean of guttural German
they never learned, or learned to disavow.
I remember hourly parades under the lindens,
the elders' white beards, the sad depths of their eyes.

I remember their talk of the North Sea,
the Rhine of Lorelei, Cologne's
twin towers, the Black Forest, the mountains,
the Hamelin piper who led everyone's children to nowhere.

But I, too, was a child: all those years
there was one word I never heard,
one name never mentioned.

SCENE TWO: Belsen

Man looks down at his map and traces a route with his finger; finds Belsen.

MAN:
I do not think I will ever live a fall day when I do not
think of Belsen.
I will be driving to work, or opening a window,
or playing cards with friends, or reading,
and I will think of Erika blowing green
or blooming violet-red over the dead at Belsen.
And I will always remember
speaking to the caretaker there.

When spring breaks, he tills the soil or
replaces a brick along a walk or transplants a tree
or rakes through the Erika and finds

a rusty spoon,
or a tin cup,
or a fragment of bone,
or a strand of barbed wire,

> *Caretaker's voice is heard offstage and overlaps with the Man's.*

MAN/CARETAKER:
or a piece of rotten board,

or the casing of a bullet,
or the heel of a shoe,
or a coin,

Caretaker enters from stage R, carrying or dragging a sack filled with small rocks. Man turns, rises, and watches the Caretaker.

LIGHTS: As caretaker appears, lights come up on stage R area.

CARETAKER:
or a button,
or a bit of leather
that crumbles to the touch,
or a pin,

or the twisted frames of someone's eyeglasses,
or a key,

or a wedding band…

He drops the sack on the ground, wipes his forehead with a hankerchief and sits down on the stool with his back to the audience.

LIGHTS: as he does this, the lights dim on him.

SCENE THREE: *Kristallnacht*

Man moves away from the Caretaker, crossing in front of the ladder to Upstage C area behind the bench and takes another glance at his map.

MAN:
It would do me no good to travel to Auschwitz.
It would do the dead no good, nor anyone else any good.
It would do me no good to kneel there,
me nor anyone else alive or dead any good, any good at all.

I've heard that in one oven a votive candle
whispers its flame. When I close my eyes,
I can see and feel that candle, its pitch aura,
its tongues of pitch luminiscence licking the oven's recesses.

A survivor, forty years later, crawled up into an oven and
        lay down.
What of his heart? Could it keep pumping its own pitch light
there where God's human darkness grew darkest?

Rudolf Hess praised the efficiency of these ovens.

> *The sound of a cane hitting the ground is heard
> Offstage R area. Man turns in that direction.*
>
> *Man 2 appears with cane. He carries a Hebrew
> prayer book.*

Man 2:
A Leipzig street.
Here, brownshirts
stomp their way

to the third floor,
fling open balcony doors,
shout something about

blessings from above.
Several wheel out
an upright piano,

batter it
through the balustrade.
It falls

It is still falling
to the street this day
of *Kristallmusik.*

> ***Man 2 crosses in front of the ladder and addresses
> the Man in Upstage area.***

Here, inevitably,
its wooden case
breaks open,

revealing what looks like
a glass harp,
unplaying.

> ***NS appears Stage R and stands next to the ladder.***

NS:
He came to our city,
and the people were shouting and crying.
They hailed the Fuhrer
as the deliverer.
I was in the crowd, caught

in delirium, a moving box,
pushed forward.

Closer and closer he came
in the glistening black car
through a sea of heads.
The people almost touched him,
but I could not lift my arm.
And now he was opposite me,
and he gave me a look.
It was a look of death,
there was the chill of death in his white face.

I knew it then:
he was the incarnation of death.
I felt it in my marrow.
All those who cried after him as their redeemer,
cried for death.
His look froze my heart,
and I raised my arm,
and I cried *heil.*

   NS salutes.

MAN 2:
In the city square that day,
my books were not burned.
The truth was being burned,
was it not? I was lost,

terrified by such good fortune,
& stood at conflagration's edge
pretending to cheer, & tasted
rot in the fruit of my song,

& shouted *Heil* …
determined, whatever else,
to live, & left that place in luck,
on fire, beyond redemption.

NS:
It's the Jews. It's all the Jews' fault.

NS/MAN 2:
Heil!!!

>*NS climbs up the ladder. Man2 sits down on bench, opens the prayer book and reads silently. Man crosses to platform and sits down.*
>
>*LIGHTS: lights dim on ladder area.*

SCENE FOUR: Hermann

MAN:

Hermann ... England's blue Channel was green
when you banked your plane and headed
back. But the Stuka's wing,
down which you sighted the countries you hated,
shone brilliant as medals,
didn't it? Your plane seemed
almost to be on fire, didn't it?

My Nazi uncle, you received the letters
my father still talks and wonders about—
the ones in which he told you to bail out
over England and plead insanity.
You got the letters, didn't you?
But you kept saying you'd land in London
with the rest of your squadron

in a few months, when the war was over,
of course. Of course. But they needed you
in Russia, didn't they? And the few
who bailed out there were met by peasants
with pitchforks and scythes, weren't they?
Anyway, your plane blew up, for a moment,
like a sun; your dust bailed out all over.

SCENE FIVE: After *Kristallnacht*

MAN 2:
After *Kristallnacht*, Herr Neckenauer, restorer, was over-
whelmed with work from Jewish customers:
legs broken, SS runes carved into polished surfaces,

doors hammered from cabinets, shattered glass–
"Barbarians," he cried, "to treat
furniture like this!"

> *Woman appears from Stage R, pulling a small*
> *wooden crate by a rope with a blanket inside it. As*
> *she moves, the crate bangs against the floor.*

WOMAN:
Around the corner where I lived a beautiful synagogue
    was burning.
Around the corner where I lived. Around the corner.
A beautiful synagogue. Was burning. Where I lived.
Around the corner where I lived a beautiful synagogue
    was burning….

My father came home in the evening I didn't recognize him.
He didn't want to talk and didn't talk what happened to him.
Was burning. He didn't want to talk and didn't talk.

What happened to him. A beautiful synagogue where I lived.
He didn't want to talk and didn't talk what happened to him.
We packed the little things we could carry.
My father said we didn't know where we are going who
    will live will die.
He didn't want to talk.

Woman crosses in front of the Man and sits down on Downstage platform edge. She rocks the crate as if it were a cradle.

Man rises and moves Down C.

MAN:
My father said don't ask from such things.
He didn't want to hear it what's the use,
goddamit, be quiet, & then we were or else …
What thinks you you're so smart, & he laughed.
He'd raise his hand, & threaten, but not hit.
What he did in the war: carpentry foreman
at Bethlehem Steel in Brooklyn against the Axis,
the bottom line. Germans make good Americans,
he said, but lousy Germans.

WOMAN:
My father came home in the evening I didn't recognize him.
Will they kill me. Around the corner where I lived.
What we could carry. We packed. Who will live
will die. Around the corner a beautiful synagogue …

Woman sings a verse from a Yiddish folk song.

MAN:
He smoked
three packs a day & hid behind his smoke.
His brothers were dead & the Jews never mind
& the war was over & this was America where
anything could happen & we shouldn't forget it.

LIGHTS: come up on Stage R stool area.

Caretaker turns around and begins to take rocks out of a sack.

CARETAKER:
From Belsen a crate of gold teeth,
from Dachau a mountain of shoes,
from Auschwitz a skin lampshade.
Who killed the Jews?

MAN:
Not I …

Man retreats to Upstage area and behind the bench. Caretaker follows him.

CARETAKER:
Not I, cries the typist,
not I, cries the engineer,
not I, cries Adolf Eichman
not I, cries Albert Speer.

MAN 2:
My friend Fritz Nova lost his father –
a petty official had to choose.

CARETAKER:
My friend Lou Abrahms lost his brother.
Who killed the Jews?

MAN:
Not I …

CARETAKER:
Some men signed their papers,
and some stood guard

and some herded them in,
and some dropped the pellets,
and some spread the ashes,
and some hosed the walls

and some planted the wheat,
and some poured the steel,
and some cleared the rails,
and some raised the cattle.

MAN 2:
Some smelled the smoke,
some just heard the news.

CARETAKER:
Were they Germans? Were they Nazis?
Were they human? Who killed the Jews?

WOMAN:
The stars will remember the gold,
the sun will remember the shoes,
the moon will remember the skin.
But who killed the Jews?

MAN 2:
Were they Germans? Were they Nazis?

CARETAKER:
Were they human? Who killed the Jews?

Man 2 opens the prayer book and reads.

MAN:
Morning tour of a German bakery.
The supervisor, born in maybe 1960,
guides us through the processes of operation,
past bins of salt, sugar, various flours, shoulder-high mixers
programmed by computers,
other machines to speed the labor by which thousands may
break their daily bread…

I am thinking about nothing particular, listening
in the broken German of my understanding.
Then we reach
the bank of ovens, some designed
to receive head-high carts of rolls,
some with racks of flat steel beds for loaves. I am
remembering nothing. I ask if these ovens,
if all these machines were built in Deutschland.

Yah, he answers. I ask if baking is accomplished
by electricity or gas. Gas, he answers …
& then I hear something the others do not hear,
& I am thinking things the others are not thinking.
& for once I am glad I am the only one,
for suddenly our skylight is a prayer from God, our air surely
sweet with the odor of bread.

> *Caretaker moves away from the Man, crosses to his
> stool, sits down. He takes a small notebook out of his
> pants' pocket and begins to read.*
>
> *Woman rises and crosses Downstage C.*

WOMAN:
Who is this SS who carries out a newborn,
holds him or her upside down in the sink,
turns on the water & sings, "Here you go,
little Moses, down the stream,"… & drowns the child
"Here you go,
little Moses, down the stream,"
"Here you go, little Moses, down the stream," …

> *Woman stops in front of Caretaker, waiting for a*
> *response. They look at each other in silence.*

> *Man looks up at NS at top of ladder.*

NS:
Do you not understand?
Every day ten thousand of my most valuable men die,
men irreplaceable. The best … The balance, then,
no longer balances. The parity of power in Europe
      no longer exists
if the *others* do not cease to be.
If they lived, those in the camps, those *inferiors*
what would be our Germany in a hundred years?
I am accountable to my people. To no one else.
If I am branded a bloodhound …so be it. I care
nothing for posthumous fame.

> *NS climbs off the ladder.*

You must learn to hate. I had to.

*He crosses in front of the Man and sits down on
Upstage edge of platform, his back to audience.*

SCENE SIX: The Children

**Man moves to Stage R area and leans against the ladder.
Woman sits down on bench next to Man 2.**

WOMAN:
This is Belzec–
smell the bodies
in the factories' smoke,

smell the sweet gas
in the clover and grass.

MAN 2:
This is Belzec
where the death compound's gate
proclaims in Hebrew,
"Welcome to the Jewish State."
This is Belzec.
This is SS humor.

WOMAN:
Curse them forever
in their black Valhalla.

CARETAKER:
As the Nazis entered the ghetto, we tried to hide the children.
What sleep drugs we had for them, to quiet them in their hiding
places when the Nazis came shouting and looking,

but the drugs were often too strong, or too weak. Bazunia,
four years old, began to cry in her bureau drawer. Closest, I
angled my hand in to comfort her, to quiet her,
but pressed too hard.

Later, mother passed daughter's body through a window to the garden below …to the moonlit frozen soil wherein the Nazis never found her, will never find her…will never find her….

MAN 2:
As I chew my morning cereal,
I remember the camps,
how victims tried to live on infected water,
their own diminishing bodies,
their will to bear witness.
In my fantasy, God is retroactive,
gives them one hour each day free from fear. They will call it the "angel hour."

Woman rises and moves toward Caretaker.

WOMAN:
They will each have a bowl of cereal,
wheat flakes with nuts and raisins and dates drenched in milk.
They will eat slowly when even the SS must cower and whisper, *die Engelstunde …*

MAN 2:
In this way, I save so many,
as I chew my morning cereal.

Woman sits on floor next to Caretaker.

MAN:
I do not think we can save them.
 I remember, within my dream, repeating
I do not think we can save them …
I know, now, this is a city in Germany,
two years after the Crystal Night

I think ahead to the hospital, the
children.

I do not think we can save them.

MAN 2:
I came to the tall wall of the cemetery.
Near the wall was a pile of coal.
I got between the tombstones.
There I was safe for the moment.
I heard screams of the children at night.
We hid out. In the morning,
they came and searched the cemetery.
The Germans went around with machine guns.

> ***Man moves toward the bench and sits down next to
> Man 2.***

MAN:
We are here, in front of the hospital …
I carry a child under each arm,
down stairs, out to my car …
I do not think we can save them.

MAN 2:
A few more days passed.
We were five persons.
We were in the cleansing house for corpses.
The Germans searched there, too.

MAN:
I am the last driver in this procession.
Many children huddle in my car.

We have left the city. Our lights
tunnel the fog beneath arches of linden,
 toward Bremerhaven,
 toward the western shore.
I do not think we can save them.
This time, at the thought, lights
whirl in my mirror, intense
fear, and the screams of sirens.
I begin to cry, for myself, for the children …

MAN 2:
We hid in an attic three days.
Later, the deportations stopped.
We returned to the orphanage.

Nobody was there.

MAN:
Later, something brutal happened, of course, but as to this life
I had to, I woke,
and cannot, or will not, remember.
But the children, of course, were murdered, their graves lost,
their names lost,
even those two faces lost to me. Still,
this morning, inside the engine of my body, for once, as I wept
and breathed deep,
relief, waves of relief, as though the dreamed
rose would spill its petals forever.
I prayed thanks. For one night, at least,
I tried to save the children,
to keep them safe in my own body,
and knew I would again. Amen.

Man crosses himself. The Caretaker approaches the Man.

CARETAKER:
I was working on his toilet.
Schwammberger came home
and took his jacket off,
and you know what came out?
A cross on a chain.

I was surprised to see this.
It fell out underneath his shirt
when he bent over washing himself.
Killing Jews with a cross around his neck.

To him it was normal, see?

Caretaker makes the sign of the cross across Man's chest, pressing his finger in vehemently.   Man moves away and crosses to USL area. Caretaker sits down next to Man2 on bench, takes out his notebook and reads.

SCENE SEVEN: SS Today

WOMAN:
Here you go, little Moses, down the stream…
here you go … Who is this SS …

> *NS rises on platform and turns front.*

NS:
Today, as SS, I rededicate myself to you,
Mein Fuhrer: I believe in you,
I will wait for you, I will follow you.
I believe in you,
I will wait for you,
I will follow you.

> *NS turns to the Man, who has come forward to watch*
> *NS by the platform area. He rises on platform and*
> *turns front.*

NS:
To speak it is one thing, to practice it another:
not merely imagine, but commit extinction,

commit it mercilessly –

but remain decent … this has made us hard,
this glorious page in our history

that never shall be written….

Should Germany need a tank ditch,
He shall have it, though ten thousand Russian women

perish from exhaustion …

Mercilessness. To carry this through. Glorious.
Mercilessness. Glory. For Germany. We, the SS
risen into the power of mercilessness.

> *NS moves to Upstage edge of platform and sits down,
> his back to audience. Man moves Downstage and sits
> edge of platform. He watches the survivors.*

SCENE EIGHT: Resistance

MAN 2:
Ten kilometers from Warsaw,
I arrived in Rembertow where
hundreds of Jews had lived
until the wheel turned: *Judenrein.*

You think they let themselves be taken? They would
not fill the trucks.
Men were shot trying to pull guns
from the guards' hands,

and hands of dead women
clutched hair, hair of SS guards,
blood-patched hair everywhere,
a *velt mit hor,* a field of hair.

WOMAN:
Curse them forever
in their black Valhalla …

CARETAKER:
We also killed many Germans,
because they came after us.
We kept a pistol in our hand,
this way—he shouldn't notice.
And when he came close and said
we should hold our hands up,
we killed him. At that time,
we killed fifteen Germans before
they could search us or kill us.
We killed them right away,
and we went on.

WOMAN:
Mauthausen, an SS bragged to a Frau Strasser:
"Today I killed another two inmates."
"How did you do that?" the office worker asked.
"I chased both of them into a vat of liquid manure,
threw a crate over them, and stood on top of it
until they drowned." …

Woman rises and "sees" the protruding head on the ground. She stomps on it as she speaks.

Now, here, his own head
protrudes from that manure. Yes,
I can see it. Now I want to step on it.
Yes, I have stepped on it, he is choking.
S, I say, S, you SS Aryan bastard,
& heel my weight on this sadist's *Kopf*
 until he disappears.

Woman sits down on the stool.

SCENE NINE: Numbers

The Caretaker reads from his notebook.

CARETAKER:
Something happened: this is history,
of course. Example:
November 17th, 1943, at Terezin,

day of the infamous census,
the SS inventing a need to know
how many Jews they had, herding
maybe 40,000 into a muddy field

to wait all day without food or water. Planes
circled overhead. Machine guns guarded the edges,
an evening of shrieking children.

At midnight,
Jews ordered back to barracks,
never mind 300 dead
This is the census:
the lost are too many,
and are lost.

>   *Man 2 begins praying, reciting the Kadish.*

MAN 2:
Yitgadal v'yitkadash sh'mei raba.
B'alma di v'ra chirutei,
v'yamlich malchutei,
b'chayeichon uv'yomeichon
uv'chayei d'chol beit Yisrael,
baagala uviz'man kariv. V'im'ru …

As Caretake begins to speak, Man 2 rises and moves away to Downstage R area, increasing the volume of his prayer. The Caretaker follows him.

CARETAKER:
In June 1941 at Bialystock,
Poland, 700 Jews were locked
into their synagogue which was then
set on fire. A German police battalion (*Ordnungspolizei*)
ringed this scene,

rifles ready in case someone
might burst out through a window, or a wall collapse
to allow even a child
any chance of survival.
In late June 1942, SS guards,
bored, ravenous for sport,
drove dozens of Jews up
from the Mauthausen pit, 186 steps,

jabbed them with rifle butts
until they plunged over the edge.
These SS wits were heard to shout
"Achtung, parachutists!"

MAN 2:
Y'hei sh'mei raba m'varach
l'alam ul'almei almaya.
Yitbarach v'yishtabach v'yitpaar
v'yitromam v'yitnasei …

Caretaker places his notebook with open page on top of the prayer book, pointing to section he wants Man 2 to read aloud.

Signed by Franz Paul Stangl, Commandant,
there is in Berlin a document,
an order of transmittal from Treblinka

248 freight cars of clothing,
400,000 gold watches,
25 freight cars of women's hair.

Some clothing was kept, some pulped for paper.
The finest watches were never melted down.
All the women's hair was used for mattresses, or dolls.

*Caretaker takes his notebook and moves to Upstage R
area by ladder. After a while, he climbs up the
ladder. Man 2 closes his prayer book and moves
toward Stage R area. He stands there, his back to
audience.*

SCENE TEN: Trains

MAN:
My mother-in-law remembered
waiting for her *Wehrmacht* husband
inside a station near Berlin.
A locomotive thundered in
hauling a dozen cattlecars.
She thought—she was not sure—
that through the waiting room's glass
she heard people moaning.
She tried to exit to the platform,
but guards kept civilians inside.
She did not smell anything unusual,
she told me, but did see hands
beseeching the air through slats....

Inside the station, for several minutes,
an atmosphere of extreme tension
until the train departed....
Later, her husband, future Stalingrader,
said that, yes, those were Jews
who preceded his own arrival,
one of many shipments to come.
He explained that, on this matter,
he forbade discussion.
She remembered that occasion
by his gift to her, a necklace
of expensive amber beads
with sea creatures caught in Time....

WOMAN:
Treblinka. Clothing, time in gold watches,
women's hair for mattresses and dolls' heads.

Treblinka. The trains from Treblinka.

Woman moves toward Man 2

Evening. This lamp glows softly,
gives off barelyenough light to read by.
You and I are children, reading a book
by the light of that lamp. We are
reading a story from a new Bible. We are as quiet as
the shadows. In the story, a master orders the
children to come to him. They leave their trains at a
station where a clock is painted on false walls.
It is always three o'clock.
The master welcomes them.
In two hours, at three o'clock, the children are ashes.

> ***Man 2 crosses to the stool and sits down. Woman sits
> on floor next to him.***

SCENE ELEVEN: Darkness

LIGHTS: Cross-fade as lights dim on stage and special comes up on Stage L on platform.

NS rises on platform and Man steps toward him on stage floor, facing him. NS takes off his helmet and puts it on Man's head. Man turns around. NS places his hands on Man's shoulders. They both speak as though hypnotized, with NS urging him on.

NS:
Thirty, fifty years later,
it's getting darker …

Thirty, fifty years later. Now
The camps – I lose them –
where are they? Darker.

MAN:
If it is true
that I've always loved him.
Darker. If it is true
that nothing matters,
darker. If it is true
that I am jealous of them,
the Nazis' hooked crosses, the Jews' stripes …
He speaks inside me. Darker.

NS:
I lie on a table
in the fuhrer's bunker,
outside his chamber,
in the hall. I am waiting.

They do not see me,
dogs nor people. This
dream begins again.

MAN:
He speaks now, says, somehow,
lower,
tells me to speak to the lower power,
for once, to say,

NS/MAN:
come back, enter, I was once alive.

MAN:
Darker. The air
swims with words, hair
twines the words, numbers
along a wrist, along

a red brick shower. Darker.
Across the street, now,
a cattlecar, stalled.
The skin lampshades darken under varnish.

NS:
Can I call him back. Millions
call him back in deepest prayer,

MAN:
Darker, always
darker. SS, death's head,
oval hollow deadface hole for boot –

NS:
The heroes
all dead in the first five minutes.

MAN:
He tells me lower …

NS:
odor of cyanide's bitter almond,
the viscera smeared to the backbone
shines with it, for me
to say it all,

my hands around his neck,
mouth to mouth, my lips
to kiss his eyes to sleep.
We will taste this history together,
my friend: take a deep breath.
Take it. Smell
almond in the air.

NS/MAN:
The leader lives.

> *LIGHTS: a quick fade out on dock area and lights*
> *up as before on entire stage. Man takes helmet off*
> *and tosses it onto platform. NS picks it up, dusts it*
> *off, puts it on, and sits Upstage platform, his back to*
> *audience.*

SCENE TWELVE: Auschwitz

MAN:
It would do me no good to travel to Auschwitz.
It would do the dead no good, nor anyone else any good.

It would do me no good to kneel there,
me nor anyone else alive or dead any good, any good at all.

CARETAKER:
We still see the electrified
barbed wire fence strung
on swan-necked cement poles
bending inward over the grounds,

ash-gray, but graceful, even beautiful,
as though unintentional elegy,
as though these lines had been conceived
by an angel in its anti-world.

> ***Man moves Upstage towards Caretaker.***

MAN:
It would do me no good to kneel there,
me nor anyone else alive or dead any good, any good at all.

CARETAKER:
I want to show you, to say
"here, here it was, here."
And you'd like,
as long as you were passing time here,
to be led there, where they were,

Woman and Man2 rise and cross toward the ladder.

CARETAKER:
in threadbare coats, or coatless,
some shoeless … Here we are,
then: cold enough
for the prisoners' breath

to mist the air….
East means Auschwitz.

ARBEIT MACHT FREI

LIGHTS: *stage lighting transforms into a steely blue.*

MAN
"Work makes you free"

WOMAN
On the prisoners' night march through winter,
one saw a milk can leaning against a tree–
she ran for it, hoping there was milk in it,
but a guard caught her, struck her
to her brittle knees in the snow, then, wearily,
unstrapped his rifle from his shoulder. "Mercy,
mercy," she pleaded. He fired through her fingers
into her face, then kicked her aside, empty.

MAN 2
Washing a toilet with his prayer shawl,
a rabbi tried to pray, but his knees burned,
& a stick pressed to the base of his skull
by an SS lout had broken skin:
blood dripped from his temple curls….
But that, for now, was their fill of sport.

Dazed, the Rabbi thought of holy oil,
of water purified by prayer,
& drying the blasphemed shawl in sunlight,
as though his present were not his future.

WOMAN:
I can remember Irma Grese. I knew her personally.
I didn't know that she was called Irma Grese.

Woman moves slowly toward Down C.

After liberation, I saw her picture in the paper.
These things have been written about, how she dressed,
and what kind of face she had, so I know that it was she.
I remember her very well. She did such terrible things.
Her face, you know, was so beautiful.
Large blue eyes and beautiful golden hair.
Beautifully dressed in such a trim SS costume,
and a stick in her hand, and with a large dog.
She would come to us every day, and before she arrived,
we had to wait there, four hours for her.

From eight o'clock in the morning
we were called to camp square without washing,
without food, without anything. We had to stand there
in the rain and snow and frost, that was all the same.
Stand lined up, four or five abreast, until *she* came.

CARETAKER:
Each morning the Germans went round with guns
finishing off those no longer able to stand up.
The Germans used their rifle butts to smash
the hands of men holding their comrades upright.
The sick fell to the ground, the Germans

piled them onto carts, stripped them
of their boots and clothing, hauled them to a pit,
unloaded them *with pitchforks* and threw them
into the pit alongside the corpses. A sprinkling
of quicklime, and that was that .

> **Woman moves toward bench and sits down, her back
> to audience.**

MAN 2:
Rabbi Solomon H. remembered his son,
a nine-year old who had,
Solomon tells us,
half the book of Psalms by heart.
When he was taken to be murdered,
he was saying the Psalms from memory. Just before being
gassed, the boy said,
"I am still going to pray to God.
Maybe at the last moment we will still be saved."

> **MAN moves away from the others.**

MAN:
As I dream, a gas chamber forms.
Light awakens inside it.
Otherwise, that space is empty.
Its doors swing shut.

Gas drops in.
The gas fills the chamber.
The light is being gassed.
The killers are killing the light.

CARETAKER:
The small stone house stands by itself,
thirty meters long, thirty meters wide,
five meters high. Two small windows
with heavy bars. A lawn in front
and a wooden shack, where people undress,
to shower, they think.
They walk into the stone house.

Concrete floor and no furniture.
Maybe two hundred nozzles stick out.

Zyklon-B: bluish pellets
dropped into a gas chamber
through this hole.
The two windows and door lined with rubber.

It's a shower, all right, but gas comes out
and twists their bodies into awful shapes.
Gas does not put them quietly to sleep.
Their flesh is torn with their own or others' teeth.

> *Caretaker climbs down from ladder, crosses to stool
> and sits down.*
>
> *Woman rises from bench. She leaves the crate by the
> bench, paces Upstage for a while; then comes to
> Down C.*

WOMAN:
Was alone, was carrying her bear with her.
Was alone, was carrying her bear with her.
Was alone, was carrying her bear with her,
bear to counsel, comfort, & protect her.

Arrived with a thousand other children
given toys to keep them quiet.
Was alone, was carrying her bear with her.
Was alone, was carrying her bear with her.

In the gas, her bear clawed free of her.
In the gas, her bear clawed free of her.
She held her bear as tightly as she could,
but in the gas her bear clawed free of her.

The mind & heart of her bear are wool.
The mind & heart of her bear are wool.
Its eyes black & shiny as tiny mirrors,
her bear is stuffed with wool.

Was alone, was carrying her bear with her,
its eyes black & shiny as tiny mirrors,
its heart wool, its mind wool.
Was alone, was carrying her bear with her.

> *Woman sits on edge of platform. She sings a refrain
> from a Yiddish folk song.*
>
> *Man sits down on back part of the bench, watching
> the Woman.*
>
> *Man 2 crosses over towards the Caretaker as if to say,
> "You remember this…"*

MAN 2:
… in Auschwitz in its season
occurred at least one soccer match
between SS who ran the camp,

& SK, the *Sonderkommando*,
the Special Squad, mainly Jews

whose daily survival depended
on beating order into arrivals,
on shorning, sorting clothes,
keeping the ovens operating,
pulling corpses from the gas,

CARETAKER:
removing gold teeth, slashing
orifices for coins & gems,
disposing of ashes.

MAN 2:
Forced
to help kill their own people,
embraced & corrupted
by the satanic Aryan engine—
with these existed parity …

CARETAKER:
Come, said the SS, *today,*
we must play.

> ***(Caretaker pauses as he recalls his own role as a***
> ***Sonderkommando.)***

Their bodies were bluish red.

We dragged them out of the gas house
by hair and ears and feet
and threw them on a flat wagon.
Each wagon had room for seventy bodies.

We drove the load to the crematorium.
We stacked them at the entrance.
Flesh does not burn like wood–
it takes a long time to burn humans.
Burning seventy or eighty corpses every day–
it's slow going.
There's always a fire in the ovens.
Day and night

a whitish smoke blows out of the chimney.

> **NS picks up a whip (lying unseen behind platform.)**
> **He stands up and brandishes the whip skyward.**

NS:
I'll send you there…

> **Woman rises and paces Downstage L.**

WOMAN:
"I'll send you there," said the Lagerführer,
pointing to the chimney.
Said the Lagerführer, pointing to the chimney,
"I'll send you there."

NS:
I'll send you there…I'll send you there.

CARETAKER:
During the revolt in Crematorium I—
Auschwitz, 6 October 1944—
though an SS guard had split his head open
with the curved end of a cane,
a member of the *Sonderkommando*

drew a knife from his boot
& plunged it into the guard's chest.
In seconds, two other co-conspirators
grabbed the SS, opened the door of our oven,
& threw him headfirst into the flames.

> *Woman suddenly remembers she left crate by bench,*
> *runs to it, and retrieves crate.*

WOMAN:
Pointing to the chimney, the Lagerführer said,
"I'll send you there."
Said the Lagerführer, "I'll send you there,"
pointing to the chimney.

NS:
I'll send you there…

> *NS sits down on platform, puts whip down, with his*
> *back to audience.*

> *Woman echoes Man 2's italicized lines. Man 2*
> *crosses Downstage Center.*

MAN 2:
To witness, to
enter this
essence, this
silence, this
blue, color
of sky, wreaths
of smoke, bodies
of children blue
in their nets

of veins: a lorry
draws up at the pit
under the blue sky where
wreaths rise. These
are the children's bodies, this
our earth. Blue. *A lorry*
draws up at the pit
where children smolder. The sky
deepens into blue, its
meditation, a blue
flame, *the children*
smolder, Lord of blue,
blue chest and blue brain,
a lorry of murdered children
draws up at the pit.

Your sign, children
flaming in their rags, children
of bone-smolder, scroll
of wreaths on Your blue
bottomless sky, children
rising wreathed
to Your blue lips.

Man rises and crosses towards the platform and NS.

Man2 and Woman cross to the bench and sit down.

SCENE THIRTEEN: The Castle

MAN:
This happened … this happens…
I cannot keep it all … an end to it …

> *NS rises and addresses the Man.*

NS:
Gaze down at the Rhine.
I remember it red
with Roman blood.

We have always lived in this castle .

> *He steps off platform and crosses in front of the Man to Downstage C.*

This is the room of trophies;
deer, griffin, boar, bear,
the long hair
and leathery scalp of a chinawoman.
Dragon, wolf, lampshade of jewskin.
We have always lived in this castle.

> *NS crosses to Stage R.*

At the base of this stair, a door
opens to the Fuhrer's chamber.
In its center stand
candelabras of eternal flames.

We had thought to leave here,
but the labyrinthine passages,

the sheer plunge to the river,
the stones that have come to caress us ...

> *NS begins to climb up the ladder.*

This is the hall once lined
by hearts impaled on pikes.
These are the stair rails
of russian bone.
This is the turret
where the books are burned.
We have always lived in this castle .

MAN:
We have always lived in this castle .

> *NS smiles and sings first verse of "Lili Marlene" and
> whistles the rest.*

SCENE FOURTEEN: Remember

Caretaker rises, picks up the sack and crosses toward the platform. He takes a rock out of the sack and places it on the edge of platform in a straight line as he identifies each population killed.   Man climbs up on platform and watches this action.

CARETAKER:
We cannot keep it all …

the Jew, gypsy, lunatic, Slav, syphilitic, homosexual,

WOMAN:
We cannot keep it all …
the German who did the shooting sitting at the edge,
his gun on his knees, and he's smoking a cigarette,
as more naked victims descend steps cut in the pit's clay,
clamber over the heads of those already dead there,
and lay themselves down.

He heard some speak
in low voice …listen …

NS:
You must learn to hate. I had to.

MAN 2:
we cannot keep it all…
Anne Frank in Belsen, jackboots, Krupp, bodies wedged
tightly on top of one another,
some still moving, lifting arms to show life …

CARETAKER:
and we knew they were all dead, said Hoess of Auschwitz,
when the screaming stopped ...

> *Caretaker crosses back to his stool, drops the sack on*
> *the floor. He begins to create a rockpile from the*
> *remaining rocks.*

NS:
Mercilessness. Glorious. Mercilessness. Glory. For Germany.

MAN;
Ist das die deutsche Kultur?
this vomit at last this last
cleansing and an end to it,
if it is possible, if I will it now.

if I will it now ...an end to it …

NS:
The leader lives.

MAN:
his will be done, and kill them, something deeper dying,
but kill them, cognac and nightmares but kill them,
Eichmann's "units" … the visions

while trains kept coming, families with
photograph albums falling out of the cars, the books
of the camps and prisons, the albums imprinting the air

as now millions approach, these trucks...arriving with more,
these trains arriving with more, from *Prinze Albrecht Strasse,*
from the mental strain on Ohlendorf's men,
from the ravine at Babi Yar, from the future,

from the pond at Auschwitz and the clouds of ash,
from numberless mass graves where Xian prayer and Kaddish
now slow into undersong …

Man kneels down by the rocks.

Woman rises and approaches the Man.

WOMAN:
A survivor, years later, allowed himself to wonder
where the dead were,
all those hanged from beams in their own barns
or slaughtered against walls
or herded to their own orchards, shot into ditches,

or starved in cattlecars to camps,
who screamed for God in the agony showers,

who burned their ways into graves in the empty sky...

But then, at last, he saw one, one thin woman in a cloud
in a blue dress wisping away from her,
dress he'd bought her fifty years before.

Man 2 rises and moves next to the Woman.

"*There* you are,"

MAN 2:
"*There* you are … "

All are looking up at the sky, imagining the dead floating above their heads.

"there," and "there," as others appeared from the west
in bursts of sunlight and cloud,

whole families of them, streets and villages of them,
cities of them, clothed in vapor, returned

by rails of sunlight, by sweeps of cloud, in carriages
of burnished cloud.

WOMAN:
 "Here, here I am, *here,"*

MAN 2:
"Here, here I am, *here…"*

CARETAKER:
"Here I am."

> *LIGHTS: lights begin to dim everywhere except on Man standing on dock area.*

MAN
O Deutschland, my soul, this soil resettled forever here,
remembered …
the families ... the children ...

the visions ...
the visions ...

> *LIGHTS: all lights fade out slowly.*

* * * * *

About the Authors

June Prager serves as Artistic Director of the Mirage Theatre Company based in New York City. She has directed Off-Broadway, Equity Showcase productions, and staged readings of many plays, in New York and regional theatres. In Philadelphia, she founded Theatre International Exchange, dedicated to presenting works by contemporary foreign playwrights, directing international premieres of *Panorama, Evacuation Train, The Komagata Maru Incident,* and *Boiler Room Suite.* Some of these productions toured to university theatres including Temple University, Delaware University, Villanova University, and Philadelphia Community College. Most recently, she created *Cedars,* an adaptation of Native American poetry presented at La MaMa in New York City. She directed the Mirage Theatre Company premiere of *Distant Survivors.*

William Heyen, author of more than 30 books, is Professor of English/Poet in Residence Emeritus at SUNY Brockport. A former Senior Fulbright Lecturer in American Literature in Germany, he has won NEA, Guggenheim, American Academy & Institute of Arts & Letters, and other fellowships and awards. He is the editor of *American Poets in 1976, The Generation of 2000: Contemporary American Poets*, and *September 11, 2001: American Writers Respond.* His work has appeared in over 300 periodicals including *Poetry, American Poetry Review, New Yorker, Southern Review, Kenyon Review, Ontario Review*, and in 200 anthologies. He was a finalist for the National Book Award for *Shoah Train*, published by Etruscan Press. Etruscan Press has also published his collected Holocaust poems, *The Candle*, the source for poems in *Distant Survivors. The Candle* provides notes for many of the poems dramatized here.

M N - N

Made in the USA
Middletown, DE
16 August 2017